MW00416016

This book is dedicated to all those

seeking to live their *everyday* lives

on purpose.

TABLE OF CONTENTS

INTRODUCTION

Have you ever thought about how nice it would be to work for yourself? To roll out of bed in the morning and not have to rush out the door or be on someone else's schedule? Have you tried to think of a business you could start yourself to bring in extra income? I'm betting the answer is yes. And you're not alone.

In the 21st Century we are seeing a shift. A shift towards entrepreneurship. Think *Shark Tank*, Etsy, Ebay, and the fact that 543,000 new small businesses open each month in the United States alone, according to Forbes.com. Everywhere you look, people are creating products, selling them online, and searching for the business niche that will earn them an income.

People want to work for themselves.

More and more individuals, of all ages, want to design their own life, set their own schedule, determine their own income and have the time to enjoy that income. And entrepreneurship, i.e. being your own boss, offers just that.

But true entrepreneurship is not for everyone. Not everyone has the $10,000 to $5 million it takes, according to franchising.com, to open a small business or franchise in the United States. Not everyone has the next big idea that will revolutionize how we live day in and day out. And not everyone has the desire to spend hours upon hours away from their family every week to make their business successful. But the one thing everyone DOES have, is the same 24 hours in a day … every day.

So what if there was a way to build an incredible income in the midst of your everyday life, from the daily routine you ALREADY have? What if you could …

… choose your monthly income
… choose your job or your work schedule
… be home every night with your kids
… have plenty of extra money at the end of each month
… choose where you want to live
… be completely debt free
… travel with friends or family whenever you want
… have 6 months salary in an emergency fund
… have time to coach your child's sports team
… go to the movies on a weekday with your spouse
… give generously to charities you are passionate about
… fill in the blank

You probably have a couple of these things already. But do you have ALL of them at once?

This book will show you how thousands of people ARE experiencing ALL of these at once because this book will introduce you to network marketing.

And for some of you, it will be a re-introduction that's long overdue.

So let go of any preconceived ideas and past experiences. This is the 21st Century. If you have access to this book, a great company, and a computer, you can build a significant income from your everyday routine.

You will never change your life until you

change something you do *daily*.

John C. Maxwell

Chapter 1
EVERYDAY TIME

let 2190 change your life ...

Everyone has the same 24 hours in a day. So let's start with an important question.

Do you plan to be alive in 3 years?

Hopefully the answer to this question is a resounding "Yes!" And if it's yes, then what do you picture your life looking like when that time comes?

Stop and think about it for a minute.

How old will you be?
How old will your kids be?
Where do you want to live?
Where do you want to be financially?
How do you want to be spending your days?

Now here's a second question.
How quickly did the last 3 years go by?

If you're like most people, it went by in a blur. Most people naturally assume their lives will be better in the future, but very few have practical plans in place to create that better life. And if you don't live each day, month and year on purpose, they will be gone before you know it.

So, what is 2,190 and how can it change your life?

It's the average number of SPARE HOURS each person has in the next 3 years. It's the number of spare hours YOU have. Look closely at the most recent *American Time Use Survey* below:

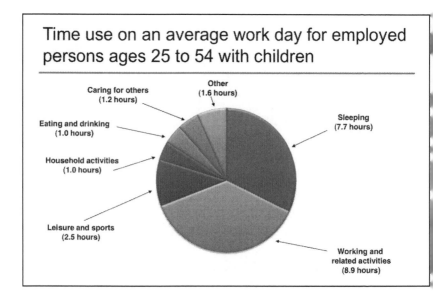

Time use on an average work day for employed persons ages 25 to 54 with children

- Caring for others (1.2 hours)
- Other (1.6 hours)
- Sleeping (7.7 hours)
- Eating and drinking (1.0 hours)
- Household activities (1.0 hours)
- Leisure and sports (2.5 hours)
- Working and related activities (8.9 hours)

This chart reveals an average day in the life of America's BUSIEST people. According to the U.S. Bureau of Labor Statistics, individuals between the ages 25-54, with children, have the LEAST amount of leisure time each day (2.5 hours). And what if you don't fall into this category? Great, then you have even more spare time.

Let's take a look at something significant.

If you take the 2.5 daily hours of 'Leisure and Sports' time and the 1.6 'Other' time allowed each day, you have a total of 4.1 hours each day that could be repurposed.

But, let's be honest, everyone needs a little 'leisure and other' time. So what if you only repurposed HALF of the spare time in the busiest person's average day. What if you took 2 hours and started making it count toward your future. If you did just that, over the course of 3 years you would have used 2,190 hours to change your life.

It might not seem like much when you first think about it, but millions of people are putting those hours to work for them a little each week and drastically changing their lives in 3 years. Thirty minutes here, sixty minutes there, week after week, they are following the blueprint in this book.

2,190 CAN CHANGE YOUR LIFE

And what if you're above average? What if you actually do have LESS time than the average person? Then this book and this business are especially for you. Busy people THRIVE in network marketing. Busy people know how to get things done. Busy people are passionate about what they are doing or they wouldn't be doing it.

And if you're NOT passionate about what you're currently doing, then why not look for a better way? Keep reading. This book will show you how to build an entirely new income stream amidst your busy life. And this book will help do some of the work for you.

Chapter 2
EVERYDAY ROUTINE

put yours to work ...

Let's put network marketing on hold for a minute and talk about you. What's your daily routine?

Day in and day out, everyone on the planet eats, drinks, showers and uses household products to get through the day. So again, what's YOUR daily routine? Does it involve any of the following:

Coffee	Shampoo	Moisturizer
Tea	Conditioner	Eye Cream
Breakfast	Hand Soap	Makeup
Lunch	Body Lotion	Hair Care
Dinner	Body Wash	Acne Care
Snacks	Baby Products	Anti-Aging
Energy Drinks	Shaving Cream	Sunscreen
Protein Shakes	Face Wash	Perfume

Take a minute and write down every single product you use on a daily and weekly basis. Add all your drinks, snacks and meals for the day too. There's probably a good chance you're not going to do it. Why? Because it would take too much time!

People around the world use dozens of personal care products and food items each and every day. Even product minimalists use between 5- 10 products every day on average. So here's the big question...

Do you plan to phase out showering in the next couple of years? Do you plan to ease up on the personal hygiene portion of your life? Hopefully not. So why not put your daily routine to work for you?

Here's how.

Find a network marketing company that provides products or services you ALREADY USE each and every day and, particularly, one with a product philosophy you believe in. Find a company with ingredients you can get behind and products that give you results.

If you're going to take a shower every day of your life, you might as well be improving your health, or at least not harming it, with the products you use. If you want to eat better, add nutrition, lose weight, or avoid food allergens, you might as well do it in the easiest way possible.

Most network marketing companies are pouring more into research and development than their retail store competitors, so they offer a higher quality product with better clinical results and finer ingredients. So choose one!

The person who gave you this book is probably partnered with one they believe in. Even if you don't end up starting your own business, chances are you will improve your health, improve your skin or add ease to your life just by becoming a product user.

So do your research.
Try the products.
Use them in your home.

After all, these everyday products are going to be a lifelong expense anyway. **Why not take the next several months, or 2,190 hours, and use them to build an income?**

And here's something important to consider if you're worried about being a salesperson.

It's important to understand the difference between network marketing and direct sales. **Please pay close attention because this might be the biggest shift you need to make to understand why so many people - who don't want to be salespeople - are jumping into network marketing.**

DIRECT SALES focuses primarily on selling products each month, which are often *not* consumable, such as jewelry and cookware. Because the products aren't consumable, it's necessary to continually find new people to purchase products and/or host parties or vendor events. The primary focus is selling a large amount of products each month, and often times these consultants are also looking for others to start their own direct sales businesses. This is not to be confused with network marketing.

NETWORK MARKETING focuses primarily on building a network of consumers that order and reorder their own personal products, most of the time straight from the company. Some of these consumers only shop online, while others build their own consumer network creating an income.

Here's how it works to create an everyday income from your everyday routine.

Chapter 3
EVERYDAY MATH

two times two equals four ...

Here's a disclaimer up front. To create an everyday income in network marketing, you'll need to be able to do second grade math. All those still feeling confident, keep reading.

Network marketing is about building a large network of people who are using their own products in their own homes. It was also mentioned earlier that it's perfectly suited for busy people. So how do you build a LARGE network of product users without turning your life upside down or having Mark Zuckerberg's social network?

MULTIPLICATION

Let's say you find a network marketing company you believe in, and you start using their products. You're thrilled to have found a quality brand and can't believe a company would pay you to be healthier, live better and help others be healthier and live better.

everyday income

You open your own business.

Look what would happen if, in your first month, you introduce someone to your company who feels the same way you do. They become your business partner. They begin using the products in their own home and following the plan. They use this book and introduce someone else to the concept of using their everyday products as a business. This pattern continues for six months.

You + 1

Month #1	You + 1 =	**2**
Month #2		**4**
Month #3		**8**
Month #4		**16**
Month #5		**32**
Month #6		**64**

In six months you'd have 64 people using the products! If they're each ordering and reordering $100 per month of their everyday products, that's $6400 in orders EVERY month in your business! And if you went one month further, there would be 128 product users just by everyone adding one more. Multiplication is the secret to having more time AND more income for everyone involved.

_____

20

But here's the real magic …

Now that you see how the math works, let's look at another situation.

Let's say in your first month you share your amazingly healthy, life-changing company with 20 people. One of them decides to join you and becomes a business partner. Five more fall in love with the products and decide to become monthly shoppers. You repeat this activity for six months and teach each new business partner to do the same. Look what would happen…

You + 1… plus 5 shoppers

Month #1	You + 1 = 2	+ 10 Shoppers	**12 Total Product Users**
Month #2	4	+ 20 Shoppers	**34**
Month #3	8	+ 40 Shoppers	**78**
Month #4	16	+ 80 Shoppers	**166**
Month #5	32	+ 160 Shoppers	**342**
Month #6	64	+ 320 Shoppers	**694**
	64	+ 630 Shoppers	**694 Total Product Users!**

In the SAME six months you would have 64 business partners PLUS 630 shoppers on your team. That's 694 product users, whether for business or pleasure. With each of them ordering the same $100 per month, your team would have $69,400 in monthly reorders! Not bad for six months work!

In ANY company that would give you a significant paycheck.

And with consumable everyday use products, your paycheck would accumulate everyday ... every time people run out and reorder.

You've just created an everyday income.

THAT is how people are building large incomes and large businesses without having to sell new products to new people their entire lives. You put in the time to lay the groundwork, build up your user network, and then continue to get paid. It's brilliant.

Of course, it's important to note that most people's businesses don't grow PERFECTLY in this manner. However, it's EQUALLY important to note that even with only HALF the results, within six months you'd have a business approaching $35,000 per month in orders. And even at THAT rate it's fun to imagine where you'll be in the next three years.

So where does this leave you?

According to the U.S. Census Bureau, there are approximately 314 million people in the United States and nearly 7 billion worldwide. So the question is, do you think you could find a couple of them who would be up for using their daily routine to change their life?

Chapter 4
EVERYDAY FACTS

two truths and a lie ...

Talking to people about network marketing is similar to playing two truths and a lie. Are you familiar with this game? People share two things about themselves that are true and one thing that's a lie, and you are supposed to identify which part is the lie. Conversations about network marketing inevitably end up as some version of this game. People share a few things they know about network marketing and at least one of them is always untrue.

People often assume that, in network marketing, the person who refers another person to the company will always earn more than that second person. It's believed that the people at the top, or the ones who got in first, make all the money. But that's the first lie.

Anyone, who starts at any time, can earn more income than those who are "above" them or those who started before them. The problem is that people picture the business as a pyramid when it's really more like a web of connected people as shown below.

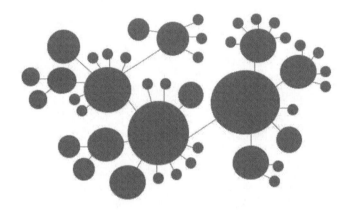

When someone starts a network marketing business, they are at the center of their own business. They are responsible for their own business but also a part of someone else's.

Any one of the circles, or business partners, could build their user network larger or at a faster pace. The person with the largest network gets paid the most, as it should be. **It doesn't matter which circle you are or when you start.**

The true beauty of this profession, that is drawing thousands in every day, is that each person only needs to use the products or services of their company and follow the blueprint for success. TRUE

When everyone does their part, the multiplication in Chapter 3 takes place. TRUE

And not only that, but you succeed and make money in this business to the degree that you help and serve others. TRUE

Finally, some of the misconceptions are cleared up. And now there's just *two truths and a truth*.

Chapter 5
EVERYDAY PURPOSE

make your mark ...

Now that you understand the brilliance and simplicity of network marketing and the significant incomes people are earning, here's the fun part. What's your dream? What are you passionate about? How can and WILL you contribute to the world around you?

Of course everyone has an immediate goal of why they start their business... pay off debt, quit their job, save for retirement, earn extra spending cash. But what about after that? What will you do once you achieve your short-term goals?

The beauty of owning your own business is YOU get to decide when and how you will contribute. And you don't have to wait until you're earning $10,000 a month to make a difference.

The world is full of need.

But the good news is that this profession has no income ceiling. Think about that for a minute… no cap on monthly or yearly income. You get to think REALLY big. And that's exactly what is ALREADY happening in this profession. People are doing amazing things with their income to serve the world because they finally have enough money AND enough time to do it.

True Network Marketers are visionaries. They are outward-focused. They are fighters. They are willing to step outside their comfort zone time and time again for something bigger than themselves, whether it's a cause they want to champion, a disease to fight, or oppression to bring awareness too. They may not always start this way, but it's a beautiful and unique by-product of the profession.

I've heard it said that, "Money in the hands of the right people is God in action."

So what's your dream?

Chapter 6
EVERYDAY PLAN

your blueprint for success ...

The purpose of this chapter is to teach you HOW to build a successful network marketing organization and build it fast if you choose.

You don't need any experience.
You don't need to know a ton of people.
You don't need a ton of time.
You don't need to do months of research.

You just need to find a company that offers everyday products or services that you believe in, and are already using, and then do the following 3 things.

SUCCESS TIP #1 - KEEP IT SIMPLE

Keeping it simple in network marketing is about letting the tools do some of the work for you. This book is your first tool for simplicity. You can explain everything that's in this book or you can just hand it to someone.

Over the course of building your business you will save countless hours by handing this book to someone rather than explaining it every time. If people want their lives to be different, introduce them to your company. Show them your business plan and how your company makes the multiplication come to life!

Beyond this book, continue to use your company's tools and team's tools to keep it simple. This might include a few key company documents, success stories, conference calls, videos and webinars. That's it. You need very little to build a large organization in network marketing.

It's about keeping it simple and it's also about Success Tip #2.

SUCCESS TIP #2 - GIVE IT ENOUGH TIME

The main reason people fail in network marketing is because they quit too soon. So it's actually less about failing and more about making a decision to stop trying. Another reason people quit network marketing is because they were really in direct sales, or were working their business as a direct sales business, and they became exhausted.

There is a lot of confusion surrounding direct sales and network marketing and most people think they are in network marketing or that they tried it before, when they really were in direct sales. Reread the difference in Chapter 2 to make sure you're in the business you want to be in.

Generally speaking, though, while network marketing can yield big results in 12-36 months, most people don't give it enough time to let the multiplication kick in. Take a look at the following chart that illustrates the power of small amounts compounding over time.

WOULD YOU RATHER HAVE $1 MILLION DOLLARS TODAY OR GAMBLE ON A SINGLE PENNY DOUBLED EVERY DAY FOR A MONTH?

	Day 1	$0.01
	Day 2	$0.02
	Day 3	$0.04
End Week One	**Day 7**	**$0.64**
	Day 8	$1.28
	Day 9	$2.56
	Day 10	$5.12
End Week Two	**Day 14**	**$81.92**
	Day 15	$163.84
	Day 16	$327.68
	Day 17	$655.36
End Week Three	**Day 21**	**$10,485.76**
	Day 22	$20,971.52
	Day 23	$41,943.04
	Day 24	$83,886.08
End Week Four	**Day 28**	**$1,342,177.28**
	Day 29	$2,684,354.56
	Day 30	$5,368,709.12

If you chose to wait patiently through the 30 days, you would have ended up with more than $5 million dollars in your pocket! **Five times** the reward over taking the easy way out.

But at the end of week two with a meager $81.92 to your name, you most likely would have been regretting your decision. Even on Day 22, as you approach the final stretch, the results just wouldn't seem to be there. You would be nowhere near the $1 million you gave up on day one.

The powerful principle of this illustration is that you have to hang in there through the seemingly small results in order to be around for the BIG compounding results when they happen. The biggest growth in your income is in the final three days. You have to see it growing, trust the system, and wait for it. In network marketing, this means not looking at your results after the first two weeks or first two months. Make a 12-36 month commitment and understand that the most significant growth can compound towards the end.

This is one of the hardest parts for people, but this is how you MUST view your network marketing business. The great thing about network marketing is that success is not about working constantly it's about doing the right things consistently. Give out this book and share your company consistently and the math will be on your side.

SUCCESS TIP #3 - PLUG INTO THE SUPPORT SYSTEM

Ray Kroc, founder of McDonald's Corp., once described the franchise industry as being "in business for yourself, not by yourself." And that's also what we live by in network marketing. You have all the freedom to set your own goals, decide your own schedule and determine your own income. But you have all the tools, training and support of a large organization at your fingertips.

Keep in mind that while the best part of this business is that you get to be your own boss, the hardest part of this business is that you have to be your own boss. Each company and team is a little different, but good ones have resources and support. Be on the weekly or monthly training calls and use the resources they provide.

In network marketing you have the ability to open your own turnkey business from your laptop and connect to your company, team and training all online. Of course you connect face-to-face also, but you are not bound by where you live. Your first business partner or shopper could live anywhere, and your team could live anywhere, so find them and stay plugged in.

> Coming together is a beginning.
> Keeping together is progress.
> Working together is success.
>
> - Henry Ford

CONCLUSION

Let's revisit that first question one more time.

Have you ever wondered what it would be like to work for yourself ... to run your own business around your own schedule?

You absolutely can.

Now is the time.
Make everyday count towards creating an everyday income.

DID YOU KNOW?

Network Marketing is a $34 billion dollar industry in the United States alone. By comparison, the video-gaming industry is at $22 billion, the music industry at about $15 billion and the NFL at $10 billion.

As of 2014, nearly 18 million people are registered network marketers in the United States alone.

The network marketing profession continues to grow year upon year, with more individuals earning more revenue in 2014 than any year previously.

Wellness products make up the largest sales category in the network marketing and direct sales profession.

www.dsa.org

New York Times Best-Selling Books
On Network Marketing

PAUL ZANE PILZER
American economist, New York Times best-selling author and social entrepreneur, he was an appointed economic advisor to two U.S. Presidents (1983-1989) and today advises CEOs and government officials worldwide. His books include: <u>The Next Millionaires, The Wellness Revolution</u> and <u>The Next Trillion.</u>

ROBERT KIYOSAKI
American investor, businessman, and best-selling author featured in *The Wall Street Journal, USA Today* and *The New York Times*. His books include: <u>Business of the 21st Century</u> and <u>Rich Dad Poor Dad.</u>

CHARLES W. KING
Professor of Marketing at the University of Illinois with a Doctorate in Business Administration from Harvard, Dr. King maintains an extensive consulting practice for many Fortune 500 companies. His books include: <u>The New Professionals: The Rise of Network Marketing As The Next Major Profession.</u>

EVERYDAY SUCCESS STORY

Audra Berger
former employee & mom

When I was first introduced to this business I immediately said no. My first reaction was skepticism. But then I read hundreds of success stories from my company and realized that a lot of busy people were making this work. However, my next thought was to assume it would never happen for me. After all, I had a full schedule and definitely was not a salesperson.

But then something happened that made it easy to get started. I was shown a business plan I could copy. I just needed to follow the leader one step at a time. And although I had some fear about diving into something so completely different, I knew that no one else was offering me anything better.

So I started my own business.

As a busy mom, I could only work spare hours here and there. But those first 3 months I learned an important lesson that brought huge success to my business. People everywhere wanted the same things I did ... more income and more time to enjoy their families and make an impact in the world. They were just looking for someone to show them how, and I had found it.

For the past 10 years my family has enjoyed a six-figure income from my part-time business. It's afforded us the continual freedom to choose where and how we want to live. It's allowed us to be able to give generously and think BIGGER than just making ends meet.

My advice...don't miss out on opportunities that come your way. Don't wait for life to become less hectic. It won't.

Choose, right now, to live *everyday* on purpose.

67288841R00026

Made in the USA
Columbia, SC
27 July 2019